TWENTIETH-CENTURY CENTURY LULLABY

by Cedric Mount

SAMUEL FRENCH

FOR AMATEUR PRODUCTION ENQUIRIES

UNITED KINGDOM AND WORLD
EXCLUDING NORTH AMERICA
licensing@concordtheatricals.co.uk
020-7054-7298

Each title is subject to availability from Concord Theatricals,
depending upon country of performance.

---

written permission of the publisher. No one shall share this title, or part of this title, to any social media or file hosting websites.

The moral right of Cedric Mount to be identified as author of this work has been asserted in accordance with Section 77 of the Copyright, Designs and Patents Act 1988.

USE OF COPYRIGHTED MUSIC

A licence issued by Concord Theatricals to perform this play does not include permission to use the incidental music specified in this publication. In the United Kingdom: Where the place of performance is already licensed by the PERFORMING RIGHT SOCIETY (PRS) a return of the music used must be made to them. If the place of performance is not so licensed then application should be made to PRS for Music (www.prsformusic.com). A separate and additional licence from PHONOGRAPHIC PERFORMANCE LTD (www.ppluk.com) may be needed whenever commercial recordings are used. Outside the United Kingdom: Please contact the appropriate music licensing authority in your territory for the rights to any incidental music.

USE OF COPYRIGHTED THIRD-PARTY MATERIALS

Licensees are solely responsible for obtaining formal written permission from copyright owners to use copyrighted third-party materials (e.g., artworks, logos) in the performance of this play and are strongly cautioned to do so. If no such permission is obtained by the licensee, then the licensee must use only original materials that the licensee owns and controls. Licensees are solely responsible and liable for clearances of all third-party copyrighted materials, and shall indemnify the copyright owners of the play(s) and their licensing agent, Concord Theatricals Ltd., against any costs, expenses, losses and liabilities arising from the use of such copyrighted third-party materials by licensees.

IMPORTANT BILLING AND CREDIT REQUIREMENTS

If you have obtained performance rights to this title, please refer to your licensing agreement for important billing and credit requirements.

CHARACTERS

MARY SMITH.
THE SCHOOLMASTER.
THE CLERGYMAN.
THE ANNOUNCER.
THE BUSINESS MAN.
THE BRIDE.
THE POLITICIAN.
THE MADONNA.

TWENTIETH-CENTURY
LULLABY

SCENE.—*A nursery.* MARY SMITH *is sitting by the fire-side, gently rocking to and fro the cradle in which her baby is lying. As she rocks, she sings a lullaby. The lamps have not been lit and the only light comes from the fire, which throws a warm glow on* MARY *and the cradle, and casts strange leaping shadows over the rest of the room.*

MARY (*singing*). Hush-a-bye, baby, on the tree-top,
When the wind blows, the cradle will rock.
When the bough breaks, the cradle will fall;
Down will come baby, cradle and all.

(*She peeps at the baby for a moment, and then goes on singing, more softly.*)

Hush-a-bye, baby, on the tree-top,
When the wind blows, the cradle will rock.
When the bough——

(*She peeps again, and, satisfied that the baby is asleep, stops singing. But she does not take her eyes off the child, nor get up from her stool by the cradle. And presently she begins to talk to the sleeping infant, as mothers will.*)

There's my precious ! (*She tucks him up.*) Sleep well !
And soon you'll grow up into a fine big boy, won't you, my darling ? And everyone will say : " Look at Peter Ulric Smith—isn't he the bonniest boy you ever saw ? " And then you'll go to school and the master will teach you all sorts of clever things. And you'll learn them all so quickly ! " Peter Ulric Smith," he'll say, " you've

got a brain in a million. If all my pupils were as easy to teach as you are, my job would be a pleasure," he'll say——

(*At this moment another voice—a man's—starts speaking from the other side of the room, and in a patch of light among the shadows we see the* SCHOOLMASTER *standing, dressed in mortar-board and black gown. He seems to be talking to someone we cannot see, and* MARY *takes not the slightest notice of him, but goes on whispering to her baby. The only difference is that now we cannot hear her because of the* SCHOOLMASTER'S *loud and rather sarcastic voice.*)

SCHOOLMASTER. Peter Ulric Smith! There's a name to give a boy! Did you ever hear anything like it?

(*He pauses for a second, with a rather sneering smile on his face, and in that second we hear* MARY *saying to the baby :*)

MARY. It's a very nice name, really—but you needn't tell the other boys what the " U " stands for if you don't want them to know.

SCHOOLMASTER. I could forgive the name if you had brains, but really you seem to be even more woolly-witted than most boys of your age—and that's saying a great deal. God knows why I spend my life teaching you and other brats like you, when I might be doing something really useful—sweeping the streets or coal mining, for instance. How I'm going to cram enough knowledge into your brain-box to get you through your beastly little examinations I can't imagine——

MARY (*still talking to her baby*). And my clever son's going to pass all his examinations—right at the top of the list—isn't he? Eh?

SCHOOLMASTER. Still, don't let us exaggerate the importance of examinations. The most important thing you've got to learn, Peter *Ulric* Smith, is that learning doesn't really matter a damn. Any cad can learn the sort of thing you find in books. What we want is a race of young men who can play games for the honour of the

old school—and cheat and lie a little when called upon
to do so.

MARY. Of course I want you to take an interest in
sport, too, but you will remember that lessons are more
important, won't you, my precious ? And do be careful
not to hurt yourself playing any nasty rough games——

SCHOOLMASTER.   Those are the most important things,
of course, but I expect your beastly parents will fret if I
don't teach you a whole lot of unnecessary things into
the bargain, so you'd better learn a spot of Latin as
well. Eh ? I'm damned if I really know why—except
that we always have taught a spot of Latin. And any-
way, we've got all the textbooks now, and we can't
waste 'em.

MARY. And then you must learn French—and German—and Spanish—then when you grow up you can
be a diplomat, or an ambassador, or something important
like that——

SCHOOLMASTER. Who wants to learn French and
German ? Now you listen to me ! My father went
round the world three times—and he never knew a
word of French and German—nor Spanish for that
matter. "If English is good enough for me," he used
to say, " it's good enough for these damned foreigners.
Why should I take the trouble to learn their damned
language ? It'd only give them an exaggerated idea of
their importance." That's what he used to say—and
he was right ! Now then—amo, amas, amat——

MARY. Or perhaps you'd rather go into the church ?
That would be nice, too. Then I could go to service
and listen to you preaching. You know, Peter, I think
I'd like that best of all. And then you could christen
all the little babies—just like that nice clergyman with
the white hair christened you——

(*As* MARY *goes on talking to her baby, we see the nice*
CLERGYMAN, *with the white hair. He is standing at the
other side of the room, quite near the* SCHOOLMASTER,
*and his face is lit up by the dancing light from the fire-
place, as he intones* :)

CLERGYMAN.   I baptize you, Peter Ulric, in the name of the Father, and of the Son, and of the Holy Ghost.

(*He makes a gesture with his hand as though baptizing an invisible baby.*)

MARY.   That would be nice, but I won't influence you or persuade you—I promise I won't.   My baby shall choose just what he wants to do for himself, shan't he, my precious ?

(*As* MARY *says this, another man's voice—a caressing, musical, condescending voice—begins to speak from the shadows, and then a flicker of light shows us that it is an* ANNOUNCER *in evening dress, speaking into a microphone.*)

ANNOUNCER.   Juvenile unemployment, says the Savant Committee report, issued to-day, has reached so serious a pitch that vocational training and selection can no longer safely be left to the individual or the parent.   The Committee recommends that a board of psycho-analysts and efficiency experts should be set up to examine all children of pre-employable age and determine on the career for which they are best fitted.   The report further suggests that the surplus or non-employable juvenile population should be drafted into Government instructional centres, to be trained in the art of employing enforced leisure . . .

MARY.   Of course, they do say it's hard for boys to get jobs nowadays when they leave school—but it won't be hard for my Ulric, will it, my sweet ?   You'll always be able to find a nice job——

ANNOUNCER.   Here are the latest unemployment figures.   The total number of persons unemployed at twelve noon to-day was three millions, four hundred and twenty-seven thousand, six hundred and one, an increase of one on the previous day's figures.

MARY.   And oh, my darling, when you do grow up and go out into the world, there are two things I want you always to remember——

CLERGYMAN. Put your trust in God, and love thy neighbour as thyself——

SCHOOLMASTER. Never take anything or anybody on trust. Look after Number One and do the other fellow down if necessary——

MARY. And whatever you do, always be honest and honourable—and never tell a lie——

(*On these words we hear another voice, a thick, rasping, bullying voice. And then we see the* BUSINESS MAN *to whom it belongs—a plump, florid creature, flashily dressed and smoking a fat cigar.*)

BUSINESS MAN. Now look here, Smith, you've been with us for over a year, and I don't deny you've done pretty well. You're intelligent and you've got a certain talent for organization, but that's not enough. I'm not in business for my health, and I want someone who can show results. Now, take our advertising. It's all right—artistic and all that—but it's got no punch. And it don't make our products look worth enough, if you get what I mean.

MARY. My Peter would never tell a lie, would he ? Promise me that.

BUSINESS MAN. Not strictly true ? Well, what of it ? What's that got to do with it ? People don't expect advertising to be true. And here's another thing. I've been going over the books, and I find you've been allowing far too much latitude to debtors. That's got to stop, too. Then there's that little matter of the diffused delivery agreements——

MARY. "Honesty is the best policy." That's the motto I want my big son to have——

BUSINESS MAN. What ? Sharp practice ? Now, look here, Smith, you're not a child tied to your mother's apron strings any longer. It may be sharp practice— I'm not denying it, though if you'd been someone outside the firm I'd have sued you for saying so—but sharp practice is what put me where I am to-day. And if sharp practice is necessary to keep me there, then sharp practice there's going to be, whether you like it or not.

ANNOUNCER. Here are the latest unemployment figures——

BUSINESS MAN. I may not be as well educated as you are, but I've yet to discover that honesty is the best policy—unless you're looking for the bankruptcy court.

ANNOUNCER. The total number of persons unemployed at twelve noon to-day was three millions——

BUSINESS MAN. Now look here, Smith, you're a good boy. You'll go far if you look at things my way. But I'm just putting you wise—it's got to be my way, or out! Get me?

ANNOUNCER. ——six hundred and two, an increase of two on the previous day's figures.

MARY. Then you'll be getting married and leaving your poor old mother. Oh, yes, you will! I know! But I don't mind really. . . . Well, I suppose I do in a way, but I'll try not to, for your sake. Especially if she's nice—oh, my precious one, you will be careful to pick the right girl, won't you? Then we'll have a lovely wedding, with the bride all in white satin and orange blossom and——

(*She goes on talking, but our attention is diverted by the* CLERGYMAN. *He is reading the wedding service to the* BRIDE, *who is kneeling in front of him, all in white satin and orange blossom, as* MARY *imagined her. We cannot see any bridegroom.*)

CLERGYMAN. Repeat after me. I, Judith——
BRIDE. I, Judith——
CLERGYMAN. Take thee, Peter Ulric——
BRIDE. Take thee, Peter Ulric——
CLERGYMAN. To my wedded husband——
BRIDE. To my wedded husband——
CLERGYMAN. To have and to hold from this day forward——
BRIDE. To have and to hold from this day forward

CLERGYMAN. For better, for worse——
BRIDE. For better, for worse——
CLERGYMAN. For richer, for poorer——

BRIDE. For richer, for poorer——
CLERGYMAN. In sickness and in health——
BRIDE. In sickness and in health——
CLERGYMAN. To love, cherish and to obey——
BRIDE. To love, cherish and to obey——
CLERGYMAN. Till death us do part——
BRIDE. Till death us do part——
ANNOUNCER. The number of marriages solemnized in churches during the past six months has declined by forty per cent., states a report——
CLERGYMAN. Judith and Peter, you have just taken the most solemn vows a man and a woman can take. You have sworn in God's house to love and cherish one another till death parts you. I hope you realize sincerely the true significance of that vow, and that you will fulfil it, come what may——
ANNOUNCER. On the other hand, the report records that the total number of divorces granted during the same period was more than sixty-five per cent. above the figure for the previous six months.

(*During the last six or seven speeches,* MARY *has been humming Mendelssohn's " Wedding March," as she rocks the cradle gently to and fro. Now she breaks off and speaks to the sleeping baby.*)

MARY. Then you must be very kind to her—but you must try to be firm, too. Remember, a man must always be a hero to his wife——

(*The* BRIDE *has taken off her veil and orange blossom, and now she bursts into · a tirade of abuse.*)

BRIDE. A hero ! My God ! A fine hero you'd make Why on earth I was fool enough to tie myself up to you for life I can't imagine. Look at the Robinsons—they've got a car. Look at the Browns—they've got a radiogram. Look at the Joneses — he takes his wife to Brighton every week-end.
ANNOUNCER. The report records that the total number of divorces granted during the same period——
BRIDE. Of course, it isn't your fault. Nothing's

ever your fault. As a matter of fact, that's probably true—it's the fault of the way you were brought up. You're too namby-pamby. You won't do anything I ask because you say it's unethical. And what's the result ? I have to go about looking like a scarecrow, while Mrs. Robinson has new furs, and Mrs. Brown has a chinchilla coat, and Mrs. Jones has——

ANNOUNCER. —more than sixty-five per cent. above the figure for the previous six months.

BRIDE. All right, all right. I admit I was with him. I've been with him lots of times. And you can blame me ? He's sensible. He knows which side his bread is buttered. He's got a car, and a yacht, and a bungalow by the river. He can afford to buy me a chinchilla wrap. Of course I was with him ! Well, what are you going to do about it ?

CLERGYMAN. To love, cherish and to obey, till death us do part——

BRIDE (*in a wheedling voice*). Of course, I want a divorce—but you wouldn't want to divorce *me*, would you ? You'll be nice and give me evidence, so that I can divorce you, won't you ? All the best people do it that way. You wouldn't refuse me this one thing, would you ?

MARY. And you'll never tell a lie, will you, my precious ?

BRIDE. Besides, if you divorce me, they won't let me marry Tony in a church—and I do so want a nice church wedding, with lilies and orange blossom and bridesmaids. You will do it for me, won't you ? It's the last thing I'll ever ask of you.

ANNOUNCER. In the High Court of Justice, Probate, Admiralty and Divorce Division, Lord Justice Jackson to-day made absolute the following decrees nisi : Robinson v. Robinson ; Jones v. Jones ; Brown v. Brown ; Smith v. Smith——

MARY. If anything dreadful should happen to you —like divorce or disgrace—you can always come to me. I'll stand by you. But it won't—oh, Peter, please tell me it won't——

CLERGYMAN. I should never have thought it possible !
I always looked on Peter Ulric Smith as such a nice
young fellow.

BUSINESS MAN. Send in Smith ! Smith, you're
sacked ! We don't want any divorcees here——

SCHOOLMASTER. You must admit a thing like that
lets down the school. And I'm told he even wore the
old-boy tie in court !

BUSINESS MAN. You say you weren't the guilty
party really ? It was a white lie, was it ? Well, what's
that got to do with me ? *I* told you to lie ? Maybe,
but this is the wrong sort of lie, my boy. I've got my
reputation to think of—and you can get out and *stay*
out !

ANNOUNCER. The total number of unemployed at
noon to-day was four millions——

BUSINESS MAN. That's my last word. You're
fired !

ANNOUNCER. —and sixty-seven . . . I beg your
pardon, sixty-eight. . . . The election. Speaking in
London to-day, the Prime Minister said——

(Out of the shadows comes the voice of the POLITICIAN, *and
at once a convenient flicker of light picks him out for
us.)*

POLITICIAN. My friends, this is a very solemn
moment for all of us. The twin spectres of poverty and
unemployment menace the security of our fair land.
Even the richest among us can never be sure when falling
dividends and rising taxes may not force us to dismiss
our second chauffeur, or third gardener——

MARY. Don't worry about being rich, my precious.
Money isn't everything.

POLITICIAN. There is only one way out of this
dilemma. We must take what we want, as our fathers
took it—and if the world refuses to give freely, then we
must take it by force. Our virile young men and
women are not going to be denied. They are not going
to fall below the high standards of their forefathers.
Read our glorious history and you will find on every

page an epic of heroism, a saga of glory, written in letters of blood and fire. That is the message I bring to you to-day.

MARY. Money doesn't matter. It's peace that counts. Peace is the only thing in life worth having.

POLITICIAN. This is a democratic country, and I thank God for it. The decision rests with you. You alone shall provide the answer. Pale peace with poverty in her train—or glorious war with work for men and honour for our nation ?

SCHOOLMASTER. History provides the answer—it must be war !

CLERGYMAN. When right is on our side war becomes holy—an act of devotion to God !

BUSINESS MAN. Trade follows the flag—give me war and profits !

MARY. It's peace that counts ! Peace is the only thing in life worth having.

ANNOUNCER. War has been declared !

(All of the characters except MARY *cheer loudly. From this point onward, the speeches follow one another more and more quickly ; getting louder every moment ; creating an air of tension and excitement.)*

POLITICIAN. War has been declared !

ALL. *WAR HAS BEEN DECLARED !*

ANNOUNCER. The royal trumpeters will now sound the " Advance." Stand by, please.

POLITICIAN. Men are urgently needed. We must have more men.

SCHOOLMASTER. I'm needed at home to teach the new generation about the glories of war.

CLERGYMAN. My place is to preach that this is a holy war—not to fight it.

BUSINESS MAN. Anyone can fight, but it needs a man like me to see that we make a profit out of the war.

POLITICIAN. Men are urgently needed. We must have more men.

ANNOUNCER. Men are urgently needed.

POLITICIAN. Peter Ulric Smith, your king and country need *you*.

ANNOUNCER. Peter Ulric Smith, your king and country need you.

POLITICIAN. For the glorious destiny of your nation

———

SCHOOLMASTER. For the honour of the old school——

CLERGYMAN. For the carrying out of God's immutable purposes——

BUSINESS MAN. For the sake of the profit and loss account——

ALL. Your king and country need you.

MARY. No, no! They'd never send you to war! They'd never do that, Peter!

ANNOUNCER. Here is the latest bulletin from the front. There was a sharp engagement in Zone Twenty-four this morning. Casualties were heavy, but neither side could claim any material advantage. . . .

POLITICIAN. We're doing splendidly. I am confident that victory is in sight.

SCHOOLMASTER. Our brave boys are performing wonders——

CLERGYMAN. With God on our side, we cannot fail——

BUSINESS MAN. Already our turnover has doubled

———

ANNOUNCER. Here is the first casualty list of to-day's engagement. Killed: Peter Ulric Smith——

POLITICIAN. Peter Ulric Smith! Dear, dear! A fine boy. Send a telegram of condolence to his mother

———

SCHOOLMASTER. Peter Ulric Smith! Write his name on the war memorial! What a tribute to the training of the old school! Fourteen of our boys have laid down their lives already——

CLERGYMAN. Peter Ulric Smith! Greater love hath no man than this: that a man lay down his life——

BUSINESS MAN. Peter Ulric Smith! He used to work for me, but this is the best day's work he ever did. I mean to say, look at my dividends——

ANNOUNCER. The royal trumpeters will now sound the "Last Post." . . .

(*During these speeches* MARY *has risen to her feet and she is now standing, facing the other characters. She is trembling and suddenly she shouts :*)

MARY. No! You shan't do it! Stop it, I tell you! Stop!
ALL (*like a mocking echo*). What?
MARY (*shrieking*). Stop!
ALL. Stop?
MARY. Yes, stop! It mustn't be like that! It mustn't! Is that what I've suffered agonies for? Is that the best you can give my son? If that's all the world can offer, then I'd rather kill him now—before he's had time to learn what a mockery it all is. I'd rather kill him, I tell you, than let him grow up—for that! I won't have it. Do you hear that? I won't have it.

(*All of the other characters begin to laugh derisively.* MARY *listens hopelessly for a moment. Then she shouts, despairingly.*)

Stop it! Stop it!

(*The baby in the cradle begins to cry.*)

There! Now you've wakened him.

(*She turns and picks up the child. Holding him in her arms, she turns again—to find that the others have all gone. In their place stands the* MADONNA, *a sad-faced, soft-voiced woman, dressed in a blue robe.*)

MADONNA. There! It's all right.
MARY. Who are you?
MADONNA. Just a mother, like you.
MARY. Where's your baby?
MADONNA. They killed Him.
MARY. Oh! (*She clutches her own baby more closely to her breast.*)
MADONNA. But you mustn't be afraid. I came to reassure you.

MARY. How can I help being afraid ? Didn't you hear what they said—that all my baby could look forward to was lying and cheating and despair and unhappiness and bloodshed and death ? Wouldn't you be afraid ?

MADONNA (*peeping at the baby*). But he isn't afraid. Look, he's smiling.

MARY. That's because he doesn't know. Oh, it was cruel of me to bring a baby into a world like this ! I ought never to have done it !

MADONNA. You say that because you haven't learned the true secret of motherhood.

MARY. What is that ?

MADONNA. You have to find it out for yourself. It's a strange thing, motherhood. You may be just an ordinary woman—not particularly clever, or wise, or beautiful—but your baby may be a genius, a great musician, or a poet, or a leader of men. You have to teach him everything—how to eat, and how to walk ; how to dress and how to talk—but before you know what is happening, he is teaching you. Things you've never dreamed of he will teach you. That's the strange thing about babies. They have something in them that doesn't come from you at all, but from outside. And that's the secret of motherhood—that something which makes every baby a potential leader and saviour of mankind. One day some mother somewhere will give the world a child which will put everything right. It may be you—or another mother across the street—or across the world. But whoever it is, she won't know— any more than you or I knew. Look at my Son, for instance——

MARY. But they killed Him, you said.

MADONNA. That didn't make any difference.

MARY. No difference ! I don't want my son killed.

MADONNA. He said : " I will come again." And I believe that He will—in some other mother's child. And perhaps this time the world will be ready for Him. Perhaps it is ready now, for yours——

MARY. Is *that* the secret you spoke of ?

MADONNA. Perhaps.

MARY. It's too much to hope.

MADONNA. Why? Isn't all motherhood hope?

MARY. But my baby——

MADONNA (*peeping at him again*). He's still awake.

MARY. I'll put him to bed.

(*She goes over to the cradle, puts the baby into it and tucks him up. Then she sits down by it again, in the same position as when the play opened, and begins to rock the cradle gently to and fro. The MADONNA stands just beyond the cradle, looking out into the distance, and, as MARY begins to sing her lullaby again, we can almost imagine that the MADONNA is gently rocking an invisible child in her arms.*)

(*Singing.*) Hush-a-bye, baby, on the tree-top,
When the wind blows, the cradle will rock.
When the bough breaks, the cradle will fall;
Down will come baby, cradle and all.

(*She peeps at the baby to see if he is sleeping. Then she sings, more softly.*)

Hush-a-bye, baby, on the tree-top,
When the wind blows, the cradle will rock.
When the bough breaks——

MARY *is still singing as*

The CURTAIN *slowly falls.*